£5.99

© 1998 Grandreams Limited

Published by
Grandreams Limited
435-437 Edgware Road
Little Venice
London W2 1TH

Written and designed by
Teresa Maughan

Printed in Belgium

conte

nts

Saints Alive!

Say hello to four feisty soul divas…

Just when it seemed the Spice Girls* were truly invincible – a girl group with staying power as well as girl power – along came another band and stole their thunder. Though that may be astonishing in itself, what was even more gobsmacking was it wasn't a boy band that grabbed the pop spotlight of 1998, but a group of four girls called All Saints.

Melanie Blatt, songwriter Shaznay Lewis and sisters Nicole and Natalie Appleton were refreshingly different from the in-yer-face approach of the Spice Girls*. Sophisticated, sexy soul-

mates, the girls have soared from being relative unknowns six months ago to divas with their images splashed over every men's magazine cover you care to mention. But they make great music too, so their faces can be seen on the covers of respected music magazines covering all the bases from hip-hop to pop.

All Saints certainly know where it's at and don't mind sharing it with us. They wear street clothes and sing about sexy subjects, they're raunchy, they're fun but they're serious about their music – so serious they write their own. After the success of the first single, 'I Know Where It's At', they followed it up with a soulful ballad called 'Never Ever', proving they should never ever be underestimated. It reached Number 1 after staying in the Top 10 for weeks and selling over a million copies. The girls were now on a roll.

Picking up two coveted awards at the Brit Awards* (Best Video and Best Single), All Saints are set to become the most talked-about group this year.

But if you want to know what really makes them tick, how they formed, where they are headed and what they think of stardom, then you'll find it all right here in the pages of this All Saints Special – 'cos *this* is where it's at!

Take 4 Girls

How All Saints made it from obscurity to superstardom – and beyond!

For every group that makes it to the giddy heights of *Top Of The Pops**, Number 1 and superstardom, there are another 1,000 bands who never get past the 'gigging in the garage' stage. What is it that marks those destined for success? Good looks, great personalities, sexy bods and immense style all help – but if you throw sackfuls of raw talent, fantastic vocals and heaps of musical ability into the mix, then you've got some idea of what makes a mega-group.

All Saints have all the above plus a whole load more. They're fresh, they're different. They're down-to earth, they're unfazed. They're funny, they're serious. All Saints are four girls who care about producing good sounds and having a blast while they do it, and they just happen to look like a million dollars without trying too hard. All that matters to these sexy songsters is making music so good it's bad! If it brings success, money and superstardom along the way then that's a bonus as far as they are concerned.

'We want everyone to appreciate us,' explains Mel, who insists, 'we're not in this for a quick buck. The music is very important to us,

we put our heart and soul into it, we write our own stuff. We'd like the money and fancy clothes too though!' It's this attitude that has probably been the reason why success has come relatively quickly for All Saints. With just two singles under their belts, one a Number 1, they picked up Brit Awards* for Best Single and Best Video (both for 'Never Ever'), and every magazine, TV show and newspaper is clamouring to get a piece of the All Saints action.

All Saints may have reached the higher echelons of pop superstardom…but exactly how did they get there? One minute you're reduced to living on convenience snacks ('Mel and Shaz used to live on Pot Noodle,' says Natalie) and the next you're on practically every magazine cover in WH Smith's.

The All Saints story begins nearly five years ago when Shaznay Lewis, songwriter of the quartet, met up with fellow hopeful Melanie Blatt. As a teenager, Shaznay spent most of her spare time holed up in her bedroom writing lyrics and miming along to her own recordings of other pop stars' tracks. She was determined to forge a career in music and, when only 15, began entering talent competitions – a route which led to her selection for session work, singing backing vocals for Ben from Curiosity and hip-hop artist Rodney C. It was here at the All Saints Road recording studio (now you know how they got their name!) in West London that she met Mel.

Mel was there as a Girl Friday-type figure, making tea, listening and learning anything and everything she could about making music. 'I was there for two years,' she recalls. 'What I used to do – it's completely sad, but that's not the point – is just

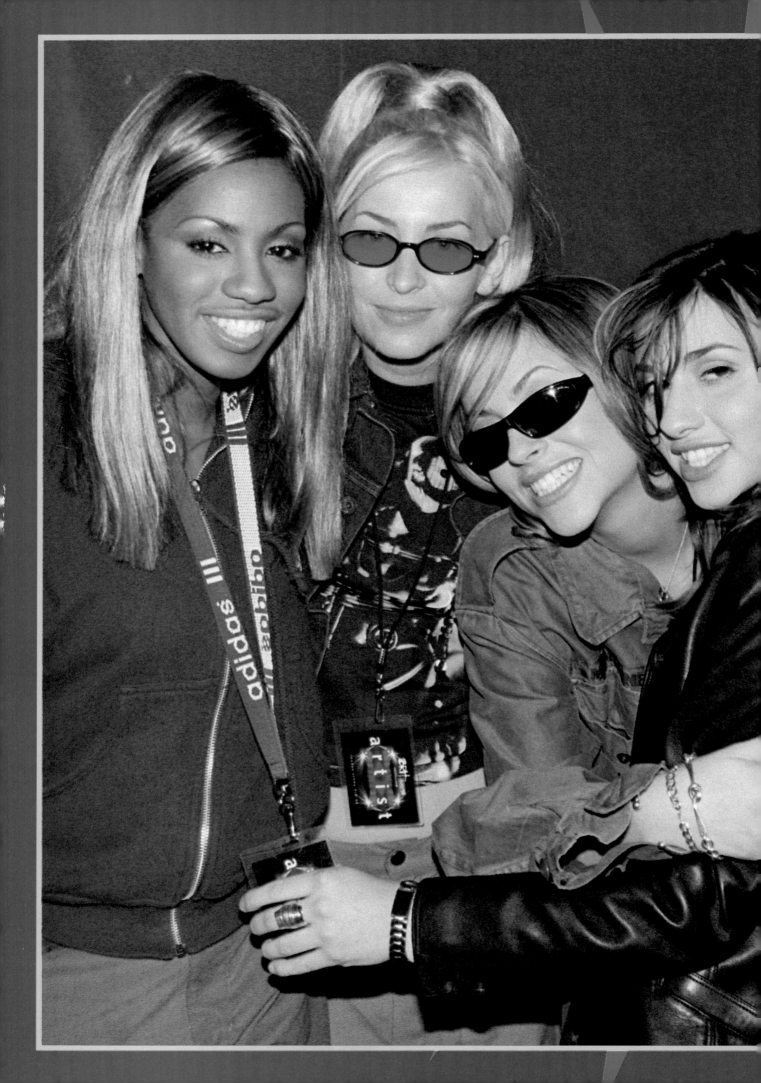

sit on the couch and listen and hear what was going on. I wouldn't ask for anything, I wasn't being paid, I was just making tea. I was nothing. Eventually I did backing vocals for people, but that was it for two years.' Now that's what you call determination! Shaznay and Mel teamed up with a third member, Simone Rainford, and formed the first incarnation of All Saints which signed with record company ZTT. Their first release, 'If You Wanna Party', didn't make it into the charts and Rainford left, leaving the two friends to think again. 'We didn't know what direction we wanted to go in and ZTT didn't know what to do with us, so it was a pretty short-lived thing. Our one release was deleted very quickly', admits Mel.

Not easily thwarted and driven with the self-belief that, when it comes to producing rockin' raunch they know where it's at, they started looking around for another group member. It just so happened that Mel bumped into old school pal Nicole Appleton – they went to the Sylvia Young Theatre school together along with 'Baby' Emma Bunton, Samantha Janus (of *Game On* fame) and Denise Van Outen. Nicole auditioned right there and then in a cafe toilet! Nicole's older sister, Natalie, was then persuaded to join, and three became four.

Armed with a demo tape hot enough to burn a hole in your combat pockets, they went in search of a deal! Despite being desperate for that big break, they courageously walked away from companies like Sony, who saw them as Spice Girl* replicas. 'Sony were interested in us, but we weren't into them,' states Mel simply. 'They just wanted us to be the Spice Girls*, which we were never gonna be.' Hooking up with manager John Benson, he brought them to the attention of London Records' big cheese Tracy Bennett, who liked what he heard and saw, declaring, 'All Saints are going to be one of the biggest bands in the world!' Seems he knew what he was talking about!

Shaz, Mel and the Appleton sisters then went about recording an album and released the first single, 'I Know Where It's At', in August 1997. Its subtle innovative mix of swingbeat, soul and funk turned people on to All Saints and it reached a more than respectable Number 4 in the charts. Next came 'Never Ever', a soulful, breathless number that overflowed with sultry sexual undertones – a steady climb to the hot spot took the quartet to the status of soul-divas and All Saints were dubbed the Queens of hip-pop. 'We've been through so much we probably should have quit ages ago,' says Mel cynically. 'The lowest point was early last year when we thought we'd got ourselves sorted just to be told, "We want you to be like the Spice Girls*." "Er, no," we said. We had to go into hiding for a bit and that was hard.' Thankfully for the girls their hard work and determination paid off – and two months after the release of the second single they walked off with two of the most prestigious Brit Awards*.

All Saints had surpassed every expectation – so overcome were they by the sheer magnitude of what they had achieved that all four members were crying their eyes out when they stepped up onstage to receive their award. 'We didn't know we were going to get any awards,' says Nic. 'Our record company had kept it secret so it would be a surprise.'

With their unique sound and refreshing attitude, the fantastic four have the ambition and drive to become one of the biggest bands this century – one with a unique talent to produce music that appeals to the music aficionado as well as to the swingbeat set. Go for it, girls!

Solo
Saint..

Full name:	Nicole Marie Appleton
Nickname:	Nic, Nicky, the Fonz or Fonzie
Date of birth:	7 December 1974
Sign of the zodiac:	Sagittarius
Colour of eyes:	Brown
Height:	5' 6"
Nationality:	Canadian
Distinguishing marks:	She's got a tattoo of the Year of the Tiger on her waist, and she's had her stomach pierced.
Lives:	Belsize Park, London
Likes:	Junk food
Dislikes:	Policemen's uniforms: 'British policemen look stupid. I'm going to make it my ambition to design one for them.'
Ambition:	'Never Ever' to reach Number 1 (an ambition realised in Jan '98!)
Early occupations:	A waitress, hotel singer, bartender and lifeguard
Musical influence:	Nic really appreciates music, particularly hip-hop. But she also loves Oasis*.
Which Saint is she?	Nic is the 'life and soul' of the group. She describes herself as 'sweet, easy-going and mad!'
Saint or Sinner?	According to Nic she's a 'saint who sins in a saintly way!'
Perfect man:	She reckons Liam Gallagher and George Clooney combined would be perfect! Nic likes men who have a crazy side, but she's attracted to mature, more sophisticated types as well.
Fave hunk:	*ER*'s George Clooney
All Saints on Nic:	'She's the crazy one of the group.'
Can't live without:	Her cats Nathan and Nathana: 'They're more dependable than any man.' She's also a walking chemist: 'I always carry Nurofen for when I'm feeling ill.'
Embarrassing moment:	Nic was working as an ice-cream seller in New York when the umbrella fell down and knocked her out cold on the pavement. 'Passers-by nicked over $90 of cool refreshments while I was lying there.'

Young, Free & Single

Being young, free and single and living in London is what most girls long for, but being young, free and single, living in London AND being in the world's biggest and sexiest pop group – well, that's the stuff of dreams...

O vernight sensations they may seem to be – but it's taken All Saints a lot of hard work and heartache to get to the heady position of sex-divas of soul. 'Because of all the years I've actually been doing this, it's made me into a bitter, twisted and cynical person,' says Mel. But even for the sexy quartet their eventual success has turned them into hot public property practically overnight. One minute they were swinging round London hanging out with mates, having a laugh and doing a job of making music, the next they were the nation's sexiest pin-ups, heralded as the queens of raunchy rap 'n soul.

With all the fame comes the inevitable change to their 'girls just having fun' lifestyles – no longer can they pick their noses in public or date who they like without it being splashed all over the

tabloids. All four girls' success has been blighted by rumours in the press. 'I hate the tabloids, I hate newspapers,' says Shaznay. 'Personally I can handle it, but I worry about my family.' Shaz admits she doesn't go out as much now because of all the attention, but despite that they're enjoying their new-found success. Nat only realised they were big when she 'saw a billboard in Shepherds Bush – it was huge!'

Relationships are often the first casualty of fame. All that jet-setting around doing promos means the Saints are never in one place for very long…and if they are, then any date they have is shared with millions of newspaper readers.

'You have to be much more discreet when you mix a love-life with fame,' says Mel, and Natalie agrees. 'Fame makes it harder to have normal relationships,' she says. 'Dating a celebrity would be a nightmare because the press could totally kill it!' She should know, 'cos she's dating Jamie Theakston!

Although the girls now get to see lots of different countries, meet loads of celebs and eat at the swankiest restaurants, they're under pressure to look good 24 hours a day – going down the chippie in a dirty tracksuit and curlers is definitely out. For Mel and Shaznay that's a big strain, 'cos they both like vegging out in old tracksuits and no make-up!

Nat used to love staying in on a Friday night when everybody else was out. 'I like nothing better than being with someone I love, with a huge bottle of wine and *Scream* on video,' she says. But there isn't much time for that kind of luxury. The last few months have been a gruelling schedule of promotional gigs, interviews and live performances and the girls have only had a couple of days off! 'That was the biggest slap in the face for me,' says Mel. 'I never knew you had to work so hard at this!'

The Saints' average working day, if there is such a thing, lasts from five in the morning until midnight! With that sort of pressure, even rock-solid friendships like theirs can feel the strain. 'We row all the time,' admits Nic.

Some things haven't changed at all, though. For instance, they still all live in the same places as they did when they weren't famous: Shaz with her mum in Islington and Mel with her parents and sister in Ladbroke Grove. 'Now I'm completely reliant on my parents again,' the Blattster laughs, adding, 'I think I might be living my life backwards – by this time next year I'll be an embryo!' Nic still lives in her flat in Belsize Park with her two cats for company, and Nat with her dad in Camden.

Opting to live at home is not without its problems, as Shaznay explains. 'The first time we did TV was for the National Lottery, and my family told me that after the show had ended all the neighbours on our street came out of their houses and started pointing at my bedroom window, saying: "That's where she sleeps!" That's just a bit *too* off-key.'

Despite the gruelling hours, lack of privacy and constant press speculation, All Saints are glad to be where they're at – it's where they've always strived to be. As Shaznay puts it when asked whether success feels good: 'Does it feel good? Man, I'm *flyin'*!' Looks like the Saints will be flying high for a long time to come…

Facing Fame

mel

With drop-dead gorgeous looks like Mel's, a little make-up goes a long way. She uses a basic matt foundation to even her skin tones. To emphasise her eyes she likes to use a soft kohl eyeliner combined with a neutral eye-shadow and lashings of mascara. 'Eyelash curlers are my favourite. I use 'em at least once a day!'

Like Nic, she doesn't use lip-liners and prefers a natural hi-gloss look for that perfect pout. To get those luscious locks Mel leaves her hair unwashed to build up a natural conditioner! Erm... yeah!

nic

With her clear, delicate complexion Nic doesn't need a lot of slap – but she makes sure she always keeps to her cleansing, toning and moisturising routine. For the odd spot she uses a concealer. She confesses to being a make-up fiend: 'I spend loads of dosh on make-up. Unfortunately it's all covered in icky dust 'cos my powder leaked in my bag – urgh!' Nic keeps her fresh-faced freckly colour natural-looking with shades of gold and brown on her eyes and a simple lip balm or gloss to maximise kissability.

All Saints have the enviable gift of being talented on the singing front as well as being gorgeous to boot – don't ya just *hate* 'em? All four exude sexy femininity and smouldering beauty. First Shaznay with her sultry dark looks and Supremes 1960s hairstyle. Mel looks like a younger, more exotic version of Dani Behr, while both Nic and Nat are two extremely glamorous blondes, Nic with her kittenish, vivacious looks and Nat with her green-eyed innocence.

You'd think that days eating junk food, travelling across the globe and constant late nights would begin to take their toll. But no sign of greasy lank hair, zits or pallid grey complexions can be seen.

These princesses of soul exude a healthy vitality and glow with energy – clear skins, perfect teeth and dazzling eyes abound. All four have that fresh-faced look that can only be achieved with subtle use of make-up – here's how they do it!

nat

Sexy Nat has men falling at her feet with her blonde locks and sultry pouting lips and she knows how to make the most of her attributes. She uses blusher for a healthy rosy glow and green eye-shadow to accentuate her eyes. To achieve that sultry look she applies a little lip-liner and fills in with a neutral glossy shade for ultimately kissable lips. To keep her shiny blonde hair looking good she uses her own recipe of conditioner – one beaten egg and a quarter pint

shaz

Shaznay has no problem with her looks. 'I've worn a brace for two years and it hasn't bothered me at all. I know it's doing me good,' she comments sensibly. Shaznay's dark skin, dark brown eyes and blonde-highlighted hair look stunning. Make-up is minimal – liquid foundation, a dusting of blusher, a natural brown shadow for the eyes, with a deep lipstick to complement the look. 'I spend the most money on foundation and lipstick from the Mac

MAY 1973

It's 14 May and Natalie Jane Appleton, Nic's older sister and Appleton kid number three, is born in her native Canada. Blonde and green-eyed, it was obvious she'd be a heartbreaker from the moment she could smile.

DECEMBER 1974

Nicole Marie Appleton made her dramatic entrance on the 7th. Canadian by birth, she is the youngest of the four Appleton sisters – and this bouncy baby, full of mischief, is still a daredevil now!

1997 was one heck of a year for All Saints, but 1998 turned out to be even better. Here's a few of the landmark dates in their lives.

It's a Date!

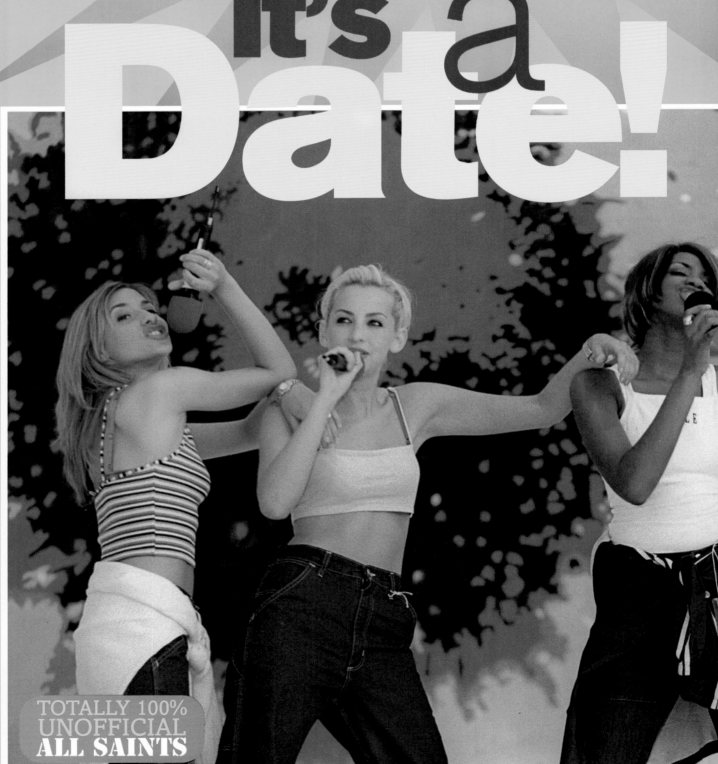

MARCH 1975

On 25 March Melanie Blatt came into the world, coincidentally in the same week Labelle's 'Lady Marmalade' was Number 1 in the charts. Her parents were French and English, making Mel a cosmopolitan girl from the instant she entered the world.

OCTOBER 1975

Autumn time, and on the 14th day of this month Shaznay Lewis was born in a London hospital. Half Jamaican and half Barbadian, music was in Shaznay's soul from the moment she started to open her mouth and bawl.

SEPTEMBER 1994

Shaznay and Mel join up with another girl and form the group All Saints. They release a single, 'If You Wanna Party', but it bombs. The third member decides to quit.

JULY 1995

Mel bumps into her old school chum Nic and they hit it off, so Nic joins the band too. Big sister Nat is encouraged to join, admitting she didn't even have to learn the song words 'cos she already liked them and had sung along.

NOVEMBER 1996

All Saints finally sign a deal with London Records after trawling around the music circuit turning down companies wanting to make them the second Spice Girls*.

JUNE 1997

London Records prepare to launch All Saints on to the UK music scene. They take a strategic decision to keep them well away from tabloids, confining them to style magazines like *The Face*, in an effort to maintain a credible build-up rather than an overnight sensation.

JULY 1997

All Saints start to make their presence known with interviews appearing in teen magazines like *Smash Hits*, *Top Of The Pops** and *Bliss*. The marketing boys at London Records are gearing up for the release of the debut single 'I Know Where It's At' and press coverage in titles like *Music Week* and *New Musical Express* mount. London Records chairman Tracy Bennett predicts All Saints are gonna be big, big, big!

AUGUST 1997

On the 18th of the month, All Saints' debut single 'I Know Where It's At' is released. A catchy hip-pop track with R&B and soul influences, it starts getting airplay and suddenly the world is interested. Trendy teen mags in the know begin to latch on to the fact that All Saints aren't your average all-girl band and can't be ignored.

SEPTEMBER 1997

All Saints reach Number 4 in the charts, an astonishing achievement for a group that had only recorded their first tracks a couple of months before. 'We were in Germany,' recalls Mel, who admits 'I couldn't believe it when the first single charted so well.' Promo-bedlam begins and a whirlwind succession of countries are visited to promote the single.

NOVEMBER 1997

The debut album, simply titled 'All Saints', is released on the 10th and reaches Number 2 in the charts. After selling over half a million copies (at the time of writing), there's no disputing that All Saints are the biggest band to emerge on the scene since the Spice Girls*. 'I Know Where It's At' gets to Number 1 in Japan and the girls jet off to perform in Tokyo. 'In Japan the fans are crazy,' explains Nic. 'I mean, they cry in front of you.'

DECEMBER 1997

The girls are about to hit paydirt with the release of their second single 'Never Ever'. With its soulful swingbeat rhythm and sexy, breathless vocals it was an immediate hit. Performances on *Top Of The Pops** followed, in fact eight in as many weeks. It steadily climbed the charts to Number 2. Hovering at this position for several weeks, the girls were robbed of the Number 1 Christmas hot spot, but success was yet to come. It was also the month that Nic and Nat were dogged by stories in the tabloid press about Nic's past involvement in a love-triangle and Nat's marriage to former dancer Carl Robinson and the fact that she has a five-year-old daughter. 'It hurts my private life has been made so public,' admitted Nic, while her sister observed, 'Everyone wants a piece of you.' December also saw the foursome travelling to Japan, Hong Kong and Paris, promoting the new album.

JANUARY 1998

This is a month the fab four are unlikely to forget. After several weeks in the charts, and sitting tantalisingly close to the top spot, 'Never Ever' finally secured that most coveted chart position – Number 1! As Nic said at the time, 'We're members of an exclusive club now!' They performed live on *Top Of The Pops** for the ninth time – their first as chart-toppers. The girls were in big demand and this month saw them packing in interviews for music and beauty mags, live performances on shows like *TFI Friday*, not to mention photographic sessions for everybody and anybody. Read the All Saints diary for a week in January and it looks like this: Monday – Denmark, Tuesday – Norway, Wednesday – Holland, Thursday – Spain, Friday – Portugal. Whew!

FEBRUARY 1998

This is proving to be a happenin' year for All Saints as they start to reap the rewards from the hard work they've put in over the last few months. At the Brit Awards* they pick up two prestigious accolades for 'Never Ever' as Best Video and Best Single. Shaz was so overcome with emotion she cried when receiving the award. She explained she'd written 'Never Ever' about her own personal experiences of heartache, 'I never thought something good would come out of something so bad!' The sexy

singers managed to perform the song with an 80-strong choir – a highlight of the awards evening. After flying off to the USA for more promo work, they were back in the UK to film the video for their next single!

MARCH 1998

The third single from the 'All Saints' album, a cover version of Labelle's 'Lady Marmalade', is released at the end of this month. The girls continue the rounds of talk shows, promo vids and magazine interviews.

APRIL 1998
A UK tour was planned, letting All Saints take their music to the public as headliners for the very first time. The pop world was at their feet – and there were still eight months of '98 to go!

25

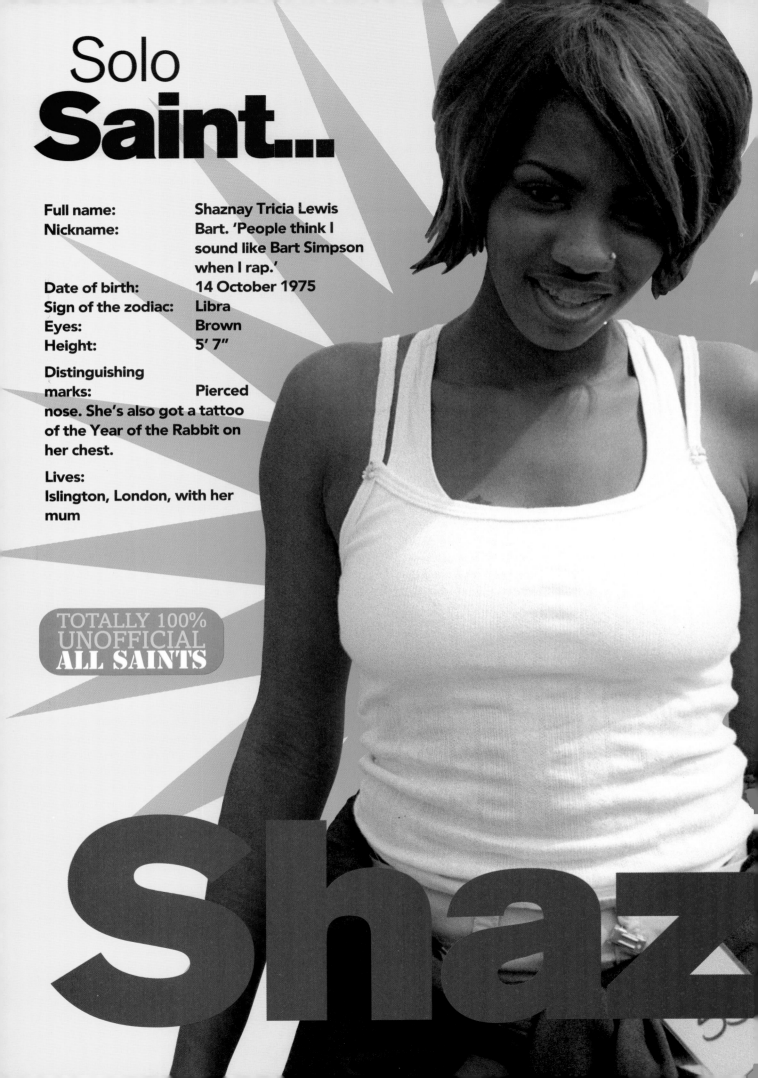

Solo
Saint...

Full name: Shaznay Tricia Lewis
Nickname: Bart. 'People think I sound like Bart Simpson when I rap.'

Date of birth: 14 October 1975
Sign of the zodiac: Libra
Eyes: Brown
Height: 5' 7"

Distinguishing marks: Pierced nose. She's also got a tattoo of the Year of the Rabbit on her chest.

Lives: Islington, London, with her mum

TOTALLY 100% UNOFFICIAL **ALL SAINTS**

Shaz

Likes:	Open-minded people who show respect
Dislikes:	The tabloids
Ambition:	For All Saints to be appreciated purely for their musical talents
Early career:	Shop assistant, session vocalist. 'I worked in a men's clothes shop for three weeks in Wood Green but I didn't have to measure inside legs!'
Favourite music:	'I'm a big rap fan, and at the moment I'm listening to Missy Elliot's album, which is really cool!'
Which Saint is she?	'I'm the quiet, shy one of the group.'
Perfect man:	Robert De Niro
What the other Saints say about her:	'She's the sexiest one in the group.'
Earliest memory:	'I remember passing my driving test!' When her examiner told her she'd passed, she was so pleased she kissed him!
Can't live without:	Underwear
Fave hunk:	Brad Pitt. 'Brad's delicious!'
Embarrassing moment:	'Once when we did a routine to undo our trousers and pull them down a bit and back up, Nic kept looking at me. I looked down to see my trousers round my knees…and, as I only had a G-string on, my whole bum was exposed!'

nay

The zodiac according to All Saints – four stars in the making!

NIC
SAGITTARIUS
Birthday: 7 December

Good Points
They're always bubbling and happy, and love having a bassin' good time.

Bad Points
Can be a bit over the top, can't sit still and are always putting their size nines in it.

Famous Sagittarians
Ryan Giggs
Brad Pitt
Zoe Ball
Jamie Theakston

Stars & The Sa

TOTALLY 100% UNOFFICIAL **ALL SAINTS**

Nic is a typical Sagittarian: she loves a good laugh, is always rushing about doing things, and is on the lookout for a bit of fun. She's vivacious, impulsive and bounces about making everyone else around her feel knackered just watching. She's got long legs, freckles and a big cheesy grin just like fellow Saggies. All Saints is made up of four fab girlies which is lucky 'cos that's Nic's star sign's lucky number!

Money management is not a Sagittarian's strong point, and they're always overdrawn. Luckily for Nic, she's now got a few bob to indulge her love of spending! Ladies born under this sign hit it off in a big way with Aries and Leos 'cos they like having as much fun as Sagittarians. Mel and Nic are such good pals because Mel is an Arian and these two signs are *très* compatible.

copping off with Shaznay 'cos these are her compatible star signs! Famous Gemini men include J from Five, football's Paul Gascoigne, Johnny Depp and Marky Mark. Well-known Aquarians include Vic Reeves, Mark Owen, Robbie Williams, Matt Dillon and, for those who fancy the older men, Peter Gabriel.

Librans hate fights and suffer fools gladly: Shaz lives up to her star sign 'cos she hates rows. Librans also love to snack, which must be the reason Shaznay loves eating crisps, pizzas and lots of naughty nibbles!

nts

Bad points
Can be vain, hate hard work and are always saying things they don't mean.
Famous Librans
Declan Donnelly
Luke and Matt Goss
Lene from Aqua
Dannii Minogue
Zac from Hanson*
Kevin from Backstreet Boys

Aries men include Damon Albarn (Blur), Elton John, Phillip Schofield and Chris Evans. Er…and Leos? How about Matt Le Blanc (*Friends*), Howie from Backstreet Boys, Patrick Swayze and Christian Slater? *That's* more like it!

Nic is a great gal to go out on a date with 'cos she's great company. But men had better beware because you can't always trust a Sagittarian – they don't mind telling porkies when it suits them.

Level-headed and sensible, with the ability to weigh up a situation before making a decision, Shaznay is a true Libran. On the downside, they can never make up their mind, are a bit on the lazy side and fancy themselves rotten! Shaz is the first to admit she's a bit of a slouch but unlike most Librans she's not scared of hard work when it's doing something she loves.

Romantic to the core, she likes nothing better than blethering on about lurve, relationships and all that fluffy malarkey. She likes her men to be romantic caring types, 'cos like her star sign she loves all that soppy, flowers, chocolates and lovey-dovey stuff! If you're an Aquarian or a Gemini you're nearly as superficial as Librans, so you stand a chance of

SHAZNAY
LIBRA
Birthday: 14 October
Good Points
They look stunning, are totally irresistible and are all charm and politeness.

MEL
ARIES

Birthday: 25 March

Good Points

They tell it like it is, they're always full of surprises and they're tops at spending their dosh on utter frivolity.

Bad Points

They are never wrong (ha-ha), they are very impatient and they can make and break promises without a second thought.

Famous Arians

Arnold Schwarzenegger
Damon Albarn (Blur)
Lisa Stansfield
Mariah Carey
'Posh' Victoria Adams

Aries is a star sign that's right up Mel's street. She loves nothing better than a good snog – in fact she admits to over 100, and those are only the ones that she regrets! She has a habit of frittering money away and, when she goes shopping, she'll buy whatever she fancies, never dreaming of waiting for the sales. In fact she can't wait for anything – she has to have everything now! That's probably why Mel, out of all the All Saints, found it so frustrating waiting for success.

Men born under the sign of the Lion are the ones she's most likely to get on with, so Leos Matt Le Blanc, Howie from Backstreet Boys, Patrick Swayze and Christian Slater look out! Sagittarians and Arians also bond well so Brad Pitt, Alan from OTT,

Ryan Giggs and Jamie Theakston are in with a chance. Shame for Mel, then, that Jamie's spoken for! But if you get involved with a Ram, be prepared for broken promises. Health food certainly isn't an Arian's bag and Mel will always choose a Big Mac over a wholesome salad. Her lucky number is seven, so maybe that's how many Number 1 singles All Saints will have this year! She'd run a mile from Virgos and Capricorns so it's just as well none of the others were born under these signs!

NAT
TAURUS

Birthday: 14 May

Good Points

Very, very sexy, cheeky, charming and completely loveable. They're also very understanding and will help anybody with their problems.

Bad Points

They're incredibly stubborn, run away and hide at the drop of a hat and can be extremely dense!

Famous Taureans

David Beckham
Mark Morrison
Janet Jackson
HRH The Queen
Joanna Lumley

Sexy Nat lives up to her strongest Taurean characteristic – too sexy for her pants! Men love her, she's always had the boys falling at her feet right from her school days. But she's a bit of a coward, like most people born under the sign of the bull, and runs a mile if things look like they're getting too heavy! Men she goes zing with are Virgos (all dependable and funny) and Capricorns (great mates and very sweet). Celeb Virgo men she might like to get to grips with include Hugh Grant, Richard Gere, Keanu Reeves and Jarvis Cocker…not a bad selection! Capricorn fellas to look for romance with include Gary Barlow, Mel Gibson, Val Kilmer and Nicky Wire. Nat's another one that lives for tasty titbits and like Mel and Shaznay has a passion for snacking. Like fellow bulls, she hates being rushed and can't stand gossip, so she's not going to like tabloid editors much! Those born under the bull love sleeping, but poor old Nat doesn't get time for that nowadays. Still, they also like singing – which is lucky for Nat, 'cos she just happens to be a singer in one of the biggest bands in the world!

Solo Saint...

Full name:	Melanie Blatt
Nickname:	Mel-odie. 'Shaznay calls me smell and Nic and Nat call me Bucket.'
Date of birth:	25 March 1975
Sign of the zodiac:	Aries
Eyes:	Brown
Height:	5' 3"

Distinguishing marks:
She's got a musical stave tattooed on her arm and a dragon tattooed across her rib cage. 'I'm a bit teed off with the old tattoo because there's only five staves on a musical score, and he's put in six!'

Lives:
Ladbroke Grove, London, with her parents

Early career:
She once worked in Kookai. 'I only lasted from 10am until 1pm.'

Favourite music:
Mel has got bags of respect for Stevie Wonder because he's influenced all her favourite artists. 'I listen to garage, R&B and hip-hop.'

Earliest memory:
Playing the viola at the Glastonbury Festival on top of her parents' car when she was six!

Can't live without:
Her mobile phone. 'It goes everywhere with me.'

Which Saint is she?
'I'm the organiser of the group. I've always got what people need in my bag – aspirin, chewing gum, whatever!'

Saint or Sinner?
She swore on *The Big Breakfast* when the group were doing a week's presenting. 'I got a reprimand afterwards. it was very bad,' admits a giggling Mel.

Likes:
Cooking and cookery programmes.

Dislikes:
Her sister's dog. 'I really hate her dog – it's horrible. It's white, fluffy and licky, and it's always trying to hump everything!'

All-time hero:
Her mum. 'She's the strongest woman I know.'

Fave Hunk:
Jay from Jamiroquai* – who, it's said, she once accosted in the street. 'He's beautiful!'

Embarrassing moment:
'After going on a sunbed I burnt my eyes 'cos I didn't wear goggles. I had to wear loads of make-up for a session we were doing the next day.'

33

Track by Track

We take a look through 'All Saints' the album, track by groovy track!

1. Never Ever

Written by Shaznay Lewis and Rickidy Raw

Inspired as a lament to a broken love affair, Shaznay wrote this a couple of years before All Saints, as they are now, got together. With lyrics that come straight from the heart and vocals that are delivered with real meaning, no wonder this sultry soul number stayed in the charts for over 13 weeks and took the top spot after a long and leisurely climb.

Full of soul swing and hip-pop harmonising, it's one of those catchy numbers you find yourself singing in the bath or humming at the shops. It's a hit that's got everything – rhythm, swing, melancholy and soul! And in case you wanted to know,

Shaznay says of her ex: 'I never got the letter but he did phone me up. I got to know some of it…but at the end of the day you still kinda blame each other.'

Sold: Over a million copies
Biggest-selling single in the Number 2 position ever.
UK chart position: 1
Rating: 10/10

2. Bootie Call

Written by Shaznay Lewis and Karl Gordon

Lispy lyrics abound in this blatantly explicit number all about erm…what it says, really! 'Bring on the rough stuff…now!' cry the Saints, proving they aren't afraid to sing dirty. It's definitely a track to get down to – a hip-pop blend of R&B and rock. 'It's about those blokes that ring you at one in the morning and ask you round to get down – it's our take on the situation,' explains Shaznay. Even Nat admits she's scared of Shaznay's lyrics, 'I'm like, "I can't sing that in front of my dad! It's embarrassing! It's *personal*! I could die!" But I do!'
Rating: 9/10 for sheer nerve

3. I Know Where It's At
(Original Mix)
Written by Lewis/Gordon/Becker/Fagen

If you wanna shake your thang then this is the funky track to party to! With an awful lot of rhythm it sure gets you swingin'. Shaznay's rap influence shines through and the inclusion of mixes by Cutfather and Jo are rockin'. 'We bring a lot of influences into our music – rap, R&B, pop, soul', says Mel. No kidding…

UK Chart position: 4
(The song made it to Number 1 in Japan!)
Rating: 10/10

4. Under The Bridge
Written by Red Hot Chilli Peppers

Classy hip-pop version of the 1992 single from the Red Hot Chilli Peppers, a strange title for the group to have chosen to cover at first glance. Its lyrics, though, are concerned with the sleazier side of life and therefore fit in well with the explicit nature of the album.

On another level, it's a summery ballad that still sounds cool and is soooo laid back. In fact it's Shaznay's mum's favourite and her daughter didn't even write it. As Shaz says, 'Cheers Mum!'
Rating: 9/10

5. Heaven

Written by the Appleton sisters, Shaznay Lewis, Melanie Blatt and Cameron McVey.
Mid-tempo pop number with a whole lot of soul. Funky and with many influences, it's a song with a broad appeal. The girls' voices harmonise beautifully, despite the fact they all have a different sound. Bound to be a sure-fire hit if they release it as a single.
Rating: 10/10

6. Alone

Written by Karl Gordon and Shaznay Lewis
'Alone' is swingbeat meets R&B with solos and harmonies running alongside each other. As the title suggests, it's about not wanting to end up alone.
Rating: 6/10

7. Let's Get Started

Written by Shaznay Lewis and Johnny Douglas
According to Shaznay this one's about the game of love: 'It's about when you first start dating someone and you're not sure what to do 'cos you don't know what the other person's like. To me it's funny 'cos it's so explicit…and it rhymes', giggles Shaznay. Real disco stuff with some wicked rap sounds from Shaznay, it's reminiscent of the 1970s' sound which is so popular now – a track Kool and the Gang would have been proud of. Got the girls into bother over uncredited sampling of the Fatback Band, but the band settled out of court.
Rating: 8/10

8. Trapped

Written by Neville Henry, Karen Gibbs, Melanie Blatt and Shaznay Lewis
Another soulful number filled with angst, this one's about being trapped in a life without love. It features some nice harmonising and lispy vocals. There is the rap influence, too, but above all it's a track that's easy to listen to.
Rating: 6/10

9. Beg

Written by Johnny Douglas, Shaznay Lewis and John Benson
Raunchy, funky and soooo groovy, it features some real sleazy vocals and some well wicked lyrics, 'On your knees and beg, beg baby!' This track epitomises what these ladies are all about…they're sexy, strong and they don't take cr*p from anybody!
Rating: 10/10

10. Lady Marmalade
Written by Bob Crewe and Kenny Nolan
'Voulez-vous couchez avec moi ce soir?' With lyrics like these it's not surprising the girls chose to cover Labelle's hit of 1975 which reached Number 1 in the week Mel was born. Funky, funky, funky – the soul sisters have recorded a version that, dare we say it, is even better than the original! Released in March, this should get to Number 1 – no trouble.
Rating: 10/10

11. Take The Key
Written by Shaznay Lewis and Karl Gordon
This is where the pace of the album shifts to a slower, more romantic feel. Lots of bass guitar in the backing track, plenty of harmonising and the inevitable rap sound, it's a track to make out to with the boy of your dreams. Oooo-ooooh!
Rating: 9/10

12. War Of Nerves
Written by Carl McVey, Magnus Fiennes and Shaznay Lewis
A soulful melody, similar in style to a Randy Crawford tune. It was written as a reflection on how Princess Diana's death brought people who hadn't experienced death before closer to the subject. Gentle harmonies with a solo that comes across with feeling – it shows the girls are talented singers.
Rating: 7/10

13. Never Ever
(Nice Hat Mix)
Re-mixed version of the original track with the girls switching singing parts and the inclusion of a funkier backing track.
Rating: 10/10

All Saints
Album released: November 1997
UK chart position: Number 2
Sold over 500,000 copies
13 tracks – most of them hit material!
Rating: 9/10

Thanks to Mel, Nic, Nat and Shaznay for a truly brilliant debut album. We can't wait for the second!

37

How All Saints became the pop world's girls on top

Number 1!

When All Saints' sexy songsters Mel, Nat, Nic and Shaz heard 'Never Ever' had finally reached Number 1 in the charts, they nearly fell off their chairs with excitement. After releasing their second single in November 1997, the girls had watched in amazement as it climbed the charts to Number 2, briefly faltering before finally doing the biz and reaching the top spot just after Christmas.

The girls hugged each other on hearing the news. 'We've been celebrating all week', grins an ecstatic Mel. 'We started on Sunday when we heard the charts! I cooked one of my special dinners for the others. It was lovely!' Nic agrees that 'Never Ever' topping the charts is the best thing that has happened to All Saints so far. 'We all got really emotional, screaming down the phone at each other. We all went to Mel's for dinner and had champagne, but it didn't really sink in until we performed it as the Number 1. It was brilliant – being Number 1 means we're members of an exclusive club now'. Too right they are! When they performed 'Never Ever' on *Top Of The Pops** for the first time as a Number 1, the audience cheered wildly and the four all left the stage with tears in their eyes. 'Oooooh, it's the most amazing feeling to be Number 1 and have everyone singing along with you', enthuses Shaz.

'Never Ever' is one of those rare singles – a proper hit with staying power. Rather than whipping up the charts in a frenzy and bombing back down as fast as Damon Hill in a racing car, it climbed in leisurely fashion to Number 2 where it stayed, tantalisingly, a hair's breadth from the

coveted top spot. After hovering there for several weeks (and loads of chewed fingernails later) the sexy quartet were rewarded with the news that it finally peaked at *numero uno* in January. Amazingly 'Never Ever' sold over 770,000 copies before reaching Number 1, more than any other single in chart history, and it stayed in the charts for over three months! What's more it had already been shown on *Top Of The Pops* * eight times before it got to Number 1, and has now sold over a million copies!

Celebrations continued with parties at pop magazine offices and suddenly the girls were in even bigger demand – if that were possible. TV appearances, photo shoots and interviews followed, and not just in the UK. 'We did Japan, Hong Kong, Paris, London and Germany all in the same week recently,' says Nat. 'We loved it!' The hard work promoting their album and singles paid off because 'All Saints' the album spent several weeks in the charts, and the singles 'Never Ever' and 'I Know Where It's At' have been hits across Europe and Asia. 'I Know…' also entered the American *Billboard* chart at Number 44.

Shaznay is cool about their success, though. 'Everyone talks about hits,' she laughs, 'like "This is a hit!" and I think, "What are you on about? I wrote a good song, man!"' This is clearly a lady who's not gonna let success go to her head: 'All we want is to get better at it. If you're ignorant and think, "Yeah, we're big and it's gonna last forever" then you're a fool and you're gonna get hurt,' opines the Shazster. So what does it feel like to finally fulfil an ambition to play on *Top Of The Pops* * with a song that's got to Number 1? Ask Mel and she says, 'It doesn't make any sense in my head at all. Only pop stars or people that are famous get to Number 1!' That's right, Mel. Only pop stars or people that are famous get to Number 1 – and that's *you*!

The Look

A do-it-yourself guide to that fabulous All Saints style

All Saints may have that 'just dropped in off the street look' that's totally unstyled and unplanned – but we all know it actually takes a lot of effort and cunning to look quite as casual as that and carry it off. Here's the gospel on how to look like you're fit for anything according to Shaznay, Nic, Nat and Mel...

NATALIE

Nat's got a sensational figure so she'd probably look glam in a bin-liner. In fact only All Saints could get away with wearing fleece-lined tracksuits and still look fabulous. Apart from the fleeces, Nat likes gear from designers like Felix Blow. 'He's really cool,' she says. She can often be seen sporting Nike trainers, Levi jackets and the so-essential shades! 'I like baggy trousers and comfortable clothes, and I love Diesel gear.'

For a swanky night out with boyfriend Jamie Theakston, sheer stockings, short leather skirt and jacket are the order of the day, and she swaps the trainers for some heels. 'I like to dress up in leather mini-skirts and look a bit more glamorous in the evening,' Nat explains.

When the girls were invited to sing at the Versace fashion show in Milan they were understandably thrilled, especially when they learnt they'd be picking up some free designer clobber. 'I got two leather jackets, a leather skirt, a blazer, a leather dress, shoes, boots, two handbags and underwear.' Nice one!

'We've always had a bit of an underwear weakness,' Nat confesses, 'but now we have an excuse 'cos everything has to match in case it's seen on stage!' Cheeky! She likes M&S* for knickers but advises, 'Don't go into the granny department.' She once spent all she had (over £700) at Macy's in Chicago!

SHAZNAY

As far as clothes are concerned, Shaznay is big on underwear. She recently left a big bag of new undies in a taxi and had to get a security guard to get it back! 'The underwear shop is the most important one to shop at!' she grins. If clothes are a passion of Shaznay's, so is shopping – she loves it when they go to New York, though she complains 'We never usually have time to shop now.'

When she does manage to nip up the high street, she heads for the Calvin Klein counter. 'I love everything by Calvin Klein because the clothes are really nice without being over the top. I also like hanging out in comfortable stuff like combat trousers – I love to slouch!' She's also a fan of DKNY and gets a lot of gear from Kensington Market in London. When the girls once took a shopping trip to Macy's in the States she emerged with bags filled with identical white trainers. 'She's hopeless!' groans an exasperated Nat. 'She buys three pairs of identical trainers – the trim was the only different feature.'

Shaz confesses she's always buying feather-lined jackets. 'I don't know how to wash the feathers so I buy a new jacket instead!' But she's a bit of a bargain-hunter, too, 'I bought a green jacket from a camping shop in Oxford Street that I'd never normally look in – it was only about a fiver!' she admits.

MELANIE

When she's buying clothes, Mel buys whatever she likes immediately and doesn't wait for the sales. DKNY is a big favourite of hers, though she loves Diesel too and has a jacket from there she nearly lost. 'I bought it in Japan and it's lovely. I wore it to MTV* once and left it there and they couldn't find it when I asked them to look for it. I went back a month later and it was still there, right in the spot where I'd left it!' she recalls. 'They hadn't even looked!'

Another big favourite is a leather coat, 'because it's really comfy and I can wear it anywhere.' Mel confesses she never looks at the care labels in the shop. 'I wait till I get home and then notice it says "dry clean or hand wash in cold water."' But, like most of us, she's also a bit lazy when it comes to looking fashionable all the time.

'It's a bit of a struggle when I don't wanna wear nice clothes,' she explains. 'Every time I come in I'm in my tracksuit and not doing anything with my hair and just putting a bit of blusher on, I'm frowned upon for not making an effort.' Cropped tops are now a favourite so she can show off her ultimate fashion accessory – a dragon tattoo spiralling down her ribcage!

NICOLE

Nic has some great assets – and doesn't mind displaying them either, with tight cropped tops and flashy bras. Teamed up with combat trousers and silver trainers, she exudes a sexy, streetwise style. 'I love army stuff,' she says, 'even though it's been around for years. I love trainers, too!' If she's going out on the town, she picks sleek dazzling dresses with sequins and stuff – or sometimes power dressing works. 'When I go out at night, I like wearing slick suits.'

To increase the size of her wardrobe she often purloins gear from big sis Nat. 'Natalie and I are always borrowing each other's clothes,' she says. She, too, landed a load of swanky gear after the Versace show. 'I came away with loads of suits, a leather jacket, swimming costumes, four pairs of shoes and some make-up.' When it comes to undergarments Nic favours stores like La Senza and Knickerbox. She loves shopping, but says, 'We have to wear hats and shades when we go to the shops now!'

COPY THE LOOK

Start with combat trousers, hooded tops, Puffa jackets and trainers by Nike or Adidas. Mix it all up with second-hand bargains for an individual look. Keep to only a few colours in muted tones of brown, black, greys and white for a neat co-ordinated effect. For a more glamorous evening look, swap the hooded top for a figure-hugging cropped top or slinky strappy T-shirt. Keep your make-up simple and your hair tousled. For that finishing touch, practise the smouldering look and a perfect pout! Oh, and as Mel says, 'Sunglasses are essential – I wouldn't be without my shades, especially after a late night!'

So you think you know the gospel according to All Saints? Go on, then, test your knowledge with our 30 taxing teasers!

The All Saints Megaquiz

1. Which All Saint has a tattoo of the Chinese Year of the Rabbit symbol on her chest?
a) Shaznay
b) Mel
c) Nat

2. In which country did 'I Know Where It's At' reach Number 1?
a) England
b) Japan
c) Germany

3. Which football team does Shaznay support?
a) Chelsea
b) Aston Villa
c) Tottenham Hotspur

4. What is the All Saints record label?
a) Manchester Records
b) Virgin
c) London Records

5. Which member used to wear a brace?
a) Mel
b) Shaznay
c) Nat

6. Which part of her body has Nic had pierced?
a) Nose
b) Belly button
c) Eyebrow

7. Who is Nat's perfect man?
a) Brad Pitt
b) Robert De Niro
c) George Clooney

8. Where did Shaznay and Mel first meet?
a) A recording studio
b) A bus stop
c) At a local club

9. How many tattoos does Mel have?
a) Three
b) One
c) Two

10. What nationality are Nic and Nat?
a) British
b) Canadian
c) American

11. Which All Saint had an operation on her spine?
a) Mel
b) Shaznay
c) Nic

12. How many members were there in the original All Saints?
a) Two
b) Four
c) Three

13. Which Saint loves films, especially *Some Like It Hot* and *Dirty Dancing*?
a) Mel
b) Nat
c) Shaznay

14. Who does Shaznay sound like when she raps?
a) Homer Simpson
b) Daffy Duck
c) Bart Simpson

15. Which Saint nearly lost her trousers while performing live?
a) Mel
b) Shaznay
c) Nat

16. What has Nat had tattooed on the top of her thigh?
a) A four-leaf clover
b) A butterfly
c) A red maple leaf

17. What is the track 'Bootie Call' all about?
a) Sauciness on the phone
b) Thigh-high boots
c) A burglar's haul

18. Which designer label is Mel's favourite?
a) M&S*
b) DKNY
c) Diesel

19. Which All Saint saves her best thanks on the album cover till last?
a) Shaznay
b) Nic
c) Nat

20. A tabloid once revealed that one of the All Saints has a five-year-old daughter. Which Saint is it?
a) Nic
b) Nat
c) Shaznay

21. How many performances of 'Never Ever' did the fab four do on *Top Of The Pops*?
a) Nine
b) Eight
c) Seven

22. Nic is going out with which famous celeb?
a) Robin Williams
b) Robbie Williams
c) Michael Douglas

23. Whose hotel room did the girls trash when they were performing elsewhere?
a) Public Demand
b) Public Enemy
c) Boyzone

24. Which Saint claims she is a pro at flirting?
a) Nic
b) Nat
c) Mel

25. Where did Mel once live?
a) France
b) Germany
c) America

26. How many awards did the girls pick up at the 1998 Brits*?
a) Three
b) Two
c) None

27. As a teenager, what would Shaznay do for hours in her bedroom ?
a) Paint her nails
b) Revise
c) Pretend to be famous pop stars by singing along to their songs

28. Who is All Saints' manager?
a) John Benson
b) Tracy Bennett
c) Simon Fuller

29. Three of All Saints attended the Sylvia Young Theatre School – but which ones?
a) Nic, Nat and Mel
b) Nic, Nat and Shaznay
c) Shaznay, Mel and Nic

30. What was Nic given one Valentine's Day by a baker boyfriend?
a) A heart-shaped cake
b) A dozen red roses
c) A dozen bagels dyed red

how you rated

If you scored 1-7

Oh dear…with fans like you, who needs enemies? Are you sure you support All Saints and not Southampton FC? You'd better read this book from cover to cover 'cos you haven't learnt nearly enough about your favourite pop group. And when you've done that – come back and try again!

If you scored 8-15

Okay, so you know who Mel, Nic, Nat and Shaznay are but you'll 'Never Ever' be able to call yourself an expert fan, will you? To become a really loyal fan you'll have to do better than that so put on the CD and start swotting – yes, now!

If you scored 16-25

Now that's more like it! You've followed All Saints from the start and we bet you know nearly everything about the fearsome four. But if you want to become the perfect fan you'll have to improve your knowledge just a little bit more!

If you scored 26 or over

You certainly know where it's at when it comes to our favourite swingbeat group. In fact, you probably know more about All Saints than their own mums! Are you sure your name isn't Nic, Mel, Shaznay or Nat?

Solo
Saint...

TOTALLY 100%
UNOFFICIAL
ALL SAINTS

Full name:	Natalie Jane Appleton
Nickname:	Nat or Fat Cat, 'cos she was a podgy baby!
Date of birth:	14 May 1973
Sign of the zodiac:	Taurus
Eyes:	Hazel
Height:	5' 5"
Distinguishing marks:	She's just had a Canadian maple leaf tattooed on her inner thigh. 'I was sick afterwards,' she admits.
Lives:	Camden, London
Likes:	Reading. 'I'm a bookworm and I love horror stories. But I *do* get scared!'
Dislikes:	Travelling and jet lag
Worst habit:	Belching and not tidying her room
Early career:	She used to sing in bars in the US and once had a bit part in *Grange Hill*.
Favourite music:	'I like a lot of old ballads, old-school rap and American classic rock.'
Saint or Sinner?	Sinner, definitely. 'I'm a heartbreaker. I get tired of boyfriends really quickly and dump them,' admits Nat.
Perfect man:	Her perfect guy would be Brad Pitt because 'he's quiet and really down to earth.'
What the other Saints say about her:	'Nat's the bossy-boots of the group.'
Fave hunk:	Brad Pitt. 'He does it for me every time I see him.'
Wickedest thing she's ever done:	Nat once kissed a friend's boyfriend when she was in the next room!
Can't live without:	Her moisturising cream, shades and photos of her family
Embarrassing moment:	'I was out on a date and a bird poohed on my head. I had a baseball cap in my bag so I put it on really quickly and said I had to go home!'

Boys, Boys, Boys!

When it comes to boys, All Saints attract them like bees to a honeypot, and no prizes for guessing why. But just what do the swingbeat girls look for in a man?

nic

Though Nic has been known to say 'Men are only good for burping and farting,' she's a sucker when a man makes her laugh: 'Someone who can be really smart, with a good head on their shoulders, and a nice bum! That's attractive to me.' Nic's been engaged before, but the relationship didn't work out, and now she's famous her ex spilled the beans on their love-life with all the steamy details – the rat! 'It happens to every band that comes out, to footballers, soap stars...' reckons Nic. 'We all expected something, I suppose I just didn't expect it so soon. And I *did* get upset...'

She fancies George Clooney (who doesn't?) and Johnny Vaughan from *The Big Breakfast*. She says her perfect bloke should have a great personality, and be a little bit on the edge. 'I like tattoos, so he'd have to have one of them, and he must also drive a Jeep and be an animal lover, 'cos I've got two cats.' Not much to ask? Up until a couple of months ago, Nic reckoned she hadn't had a boyfriend for two years and admitted 'I'm chewing my fingernails...no, make that my toenails, with frustration'.

She's had plenty of crushes on blokes, though, like Robbie Williams. 'We met him when we were doing *Top Of The Pops*. But I haven't got a chance. I've seen the kind of girls he goes for and they're not like me at all. They are quite naturally attractive and beautiful and I'm twice the size of half of them!' Oo-er, seems she was wrong, 'cos in early 1998 she was dating the raunchy ex-Take Thatter. But when it comes to current fellas, Nic's keeping her lips glued together.

mel

Like Nic, Mel reckons she's been celibate for a while now. 'I'm thinking about joining a nunnery,' she jests. A more serious Mel explains, 'It seems you can't have a love-life and do this!' She wouldn't snog Dean Gaffney if her life depended on it, 'he's disgusting,' and she really hates 'new age' 1990s males. 'I hate men that think they've got to be a stereotype. If men act like lads that's okay, as long as they are not doing it to be fashionable.'

But the men she hates most are the ones that are too caring. 'They make me puke!' She reckons she's got over 100 snogs on her list that she'd rather forget, and claims she's never ever been in love. Aaaah, poor Mel! Maybe it's because she's hopeless at chatting men up. 'I'm not a flirt at all – I'm really shy!'

If she had the chance, though, she'd love to date Jay Kay from Jamiroquai*. 'I jumped on him in the street and said, "I love you, we've got the same lawyers and accountants!" and he said "Well, we'll be getting married next then!" Yeesss!' She also admits to having a thing for boxer Robin Reid, 'especially when he's dripping with sweat!' Mel's had her fair share of tabloid rumours that claim she used to date dreamboat Peter Andre but she insists they've known each other for ages. 'We're just friends. Honest!' She will admit she has recently got a new boyfriend, but won't say who the lucky chap is!

shaz

Shaznay admits to 'only ever being in love once,' and says the words 'I love you' shouldn't be taken lightly. 'I think love's the nicest thing in the world – but also the most dangerous.' The most romantic thing she's ever done is ring up a radio station to get the DJ to tell her boyfriend she loved him. She had a long-term relationship with her first fella and she wrote 'Never Ever' four years ago when she was going through the pain of the break-up. 'He was my first proper boyfriend. When it all went wrong after two years, I was in such pain. I put my feelings into words in the song.'

So what type of guy turns her on? 'For me, it's the way they carry themselves. They could be really good looking, but if they don't approach me in the right way that's not cool!' She likes Robert De Niro, but isn't hooked on any one guy. 'He would have to be somebody I could have loads of fun with.' Shaznay says she's actually pleased to be having a bit of a breather from men, but with her looks we bet that state of affairs doesn't last long!

The press have already claimed Shaznay was involved with Wayne Morris from Boyz II Men but Shaznay said, 'I felt really embarrassed about that. I've know him since I was, maybe, 18 and we're really good friends.' In fact, tabloid stories are already running rife about her relationship with former Bros star Matt Goss – but shy Shaz won't say whether they're an item! Secretive or what?

nat

Nat loves boys, and makes no secret about it. 'I love men who are wise' but she hates nerdy dancers and blokes that try to impress. She confesses she's always been a heartbreaker. 'I'm such a bitch. I always end up hurting people. I get really bored and my relationships never seem to last longer then three months.' She says she's scared of getting too involved now because she was hurt when she was young.

Nat had her fair share of hurt when her marriage to a male dancer broke up. But men don't seem to let that put them off.

'People used to think I was strange, 'cos I wore men's clothes, but I still used to get all the guys!' Nat loves snogging, too. 'A good snog can really make your day,' and claims to have kissed over 45 blokes including loads of celebs. She says she's the queen of flirting. 'I just slant my mouth, squint my eyes and smile. It really works!' She confesses that she once made a move on a fella in a club and fell down the stairs – so cool! When it comes to her perfect man she goes ga-ga over Brad Pitt.

Contrary to recent press rumours, she's never dated Brad, but she has met him and now only has eyes for *Live 'n Kicking* presenter Jamie Theakston. But when questioned about the relationship, Jamie said, 'I've been out with Nat but I don't think we'd be considered girlfriend and boyfriend. We've been out a couple of times but they haven't been real dates!' All Nat will reveal is, 'Jamie is a very good friend of mine!'

All Saints versus the Spice Girls* – now *there's* a battle we've got to see!

Battle Of The Bands

Unlike boy bands, girl groups as successful as the Spice Girls* and All Saints are a relatively new phenomenon – and, with All Saints launching in the wake of the feisty five's global victory, it's inevitable comparisons will be made. In fact, being tagged 'the new Spice Girls*' is something that's dogged All Saints right from the off, and is a label they're at great pains to shake off. Mel, Shaznay, Nic and Nat all insist they're not a replica of anybody – and woe betide the record companies that tried to make them otherwise!

True they are girls, they sing, they look good, they're individuals and both groups have a member called Mel B, but that really is as far as it goes – 'cos these sassy lasses are different in a big way!

56

THE MUSIC

Where the Spice Girls* are all about catchy pop numbers with a lot of oomph, All Saints are altogether more sultry – liquid-gold vocals drizzled with steamy lyrics. If a Spice Girl* single is snogging in a Ford Escort, then an All Saints number is akin to sipping champagne in a stretch limo.

Let's look at their debut singles. Compare the brash style of 'I tell you what I want, what I really, really want' to the subtle sophistication of 'If you want to have a good time, then I know where it's at' and it's the Saints who come out on top.

ALL SAINTS 10
SPICE GIRLS* 9

SONGWRITING

We've heard all about the Spicies 'doin' it for themselves', determining their own future and writing their own music, but All Saints do it too. Shaznay has a hand in all the songs, and all four girls are heavily involved in the type of music they produce. Each brings their own hip-hop, rock, R&B and soul influence which gives their music its originality and flair. 'We're just happy the music we've been listening to for four years is finally being listened to by so many people across the world,' enthuses Shaznay, 'and that is so cool.'

ALL SAINTS 9
SPICE GIRLS* 9

SEX APPEAL

Dubbed 'the princesses of sex-soul' by *New Musical Express*, All Saints know how to deliver with their sexy pouts, smoky looks and perfectly formed bods. Their fans cover a far greater age range to their rivals, the Spicies' more upfront, in-yer-face approach attracting the younger vote.

Both sides seem to score with the football crowd, Paul 'Gazza' Gascoigne a fully paid-up admirer of the Saints fan club to rival 'Mr Posh', David Beckham. But when it comes to turning heads, the Saints are in a 'league' of their own.

ALL SAINTS 10
SPICE GIRLS* 8

THE LOOK

Move over Ginger, Sporty, Posh, Scary and Baby 'cos these girls don't need labels to be individuals. Each with their own brand of style – Mel with her sultry pout and Bardot hair-do, Nat with her blonde intelligent sophistication, Nic with her 'I'm a sinner not a saint, who gives a d*mn?' tousled look and Shaznay with her sexy but vulnerable look. All four manage to look good in anything from fleeced hoods to combats and achieve that 'just stepped out of bed, looking utterly ravishing, without even trying' look.

ALL SAINTS 10
SPICE GIRLS* 9

TABLOID APPEAL

The British press likes nothing more than to dish the dirt on anybody in the public eye and both groups have had their fair share of exposés. When the Spice Girls* broke big the public couldn't get enough of them and stories featured nearly every day on what they were up to, which parties they'd attended and who'd busted out all over! Then came the backlash – and when it comes to trees felled, we're talking whole rain forests!

All four Saints have had their private lives splattered all over the tabloids too, but figure it goes with the territory. 'You know I've hung around people it's happened to, and it's true when they say it'll be tomorrow's fish and chip paper. I don't really care,' says Nic.

ALL SAINTS 9
SPICE GIRLS* 10

GLOBAL DOMINATION

When the Spice Girls* said they were going for world domination with the Girl Power message, they meant what they said. They're undoubtedly the best-known pop group in the world right now, their appeal spanning across the continents of Asia, Africa, Europe and that notoriously hard-to-crack market, America. All Saints have already done their fair share of globetrotting, having visited most of Europe and Japan – but since they've yet to do a full tour of the UK, let alone the world, then we can safely say the Spice Girls* walk this one!

ALL SAINTS 8
SPICE GIRLS* 10

TOTAL
ALL SAINTS 56
SPICE GIRLS* 55

You heard it here first! When it comes to the battle for female supremacy Woman Power beats Girl Power by a head. Those feisty Spice Girls* may be winning in the record sales stakes, but they should start looking over their tattooed shoulders 'cos the Saints are coming up from behind…and at a racy old pace too.

As All Saints manager John Benson says, 'This is a marriage that's going to last, not just something to sleep or flirt with. They're not the new Spice Girls* or Bananarama, they'll be around for a long time!'

What they've done, where they're going

In the space of only a couple of months, Mel, Nat, Nic and Shaznay have been transformed from four ordinary good-looking girls with a passion for writing songs and having fun to four super sex-goddesses with more press pulling-power than the Royal Family. For the fab four it was a dream come true to watch their debut single climb up the charts and reach a respectable Number 4 in the UK. Next the album reached Number 2, at one point selling faster than the Spice Girls*' long-awaited second effort, and then the second single surpassed expectations by going all the way to Number 1.

All this was achieved despite, rather than because of, the success of global pop phenomenon the Spice Girls*. If anything, All Saints' achievements have been all the more amazing because they were up against the biggest girl band in the world when they released the 'All Saints' album and second single, 'Never Ever'.

The sexy quartet have achieved their goals as fast as Manchester United's* Andy Cole can score 'em. With two hugely successful singles and a stunning first album behind them, the girls all agreed being an All Saint was 'the best thing that had ever happened to them', but the best was yet to come. A double-whammy at the Brit Awards* equalled the success of the Spice Girls* and they were hotter than a Teletubbie on Christmas Eve. With further success in Europe and the States seemingly on the cards, where will the most original purveyors of hip-hop soul go from here?

Saints' Progress

Well, with the amount of interest they've had from both men's and beauty magazines, all of the girls could carve themselves out careers in modelling – they've got the looks and the figures for it. But none of the four are gonna be needing a change of job – they'll be too busy conquering the world peddling their own particular brand of hip-hop!

A good thing too, since, by Nic's own admission, 'I've been sacked from every job I've ever had!' After the UK tour, they'll want to tour throughout Europe and then it's on to the world stage. More singles will follow, all of them likely to be chartbusters, and the girls will be looking to beat the Spice Girls*' record of consecutive Number 1 singles. When they've done all that maybe All Saints will consider trying their hand at becoming silver-screen babes – there'll be no shortage of offers, that's for sure! The world is quite definitely their oyster right now, and they are the pearls.

'It'd be great to think we could be ten times bigger this time next year,' sighs a hopeful Mel. 'And if it means we become massive sex symbols, then so be it!' Yep, there's no disputing that, right now, All Saints are the princesses of swingbeat, the queens of sultry soul – and long may they reign!